DRYLONGSO

DRYLONGSO

WRITTEN BY

Virginia Hamilton

ILLUSTRATED BY

Jerry Pinkney

HOUGHTON MIFFLIN   BOSTON • MORRIS PLAINS, NJ

California • Colorado • Georgia • Illinois • New Jersey • Texas

For Leigh and Jaime
—V. H.

Hope for the conservation of the earth
—J. P.

DRYLONGSO

Lindy skipped along, leaving a trail of dust behind her. She had her wiper rag. She must wipe each plant and flower clean. For red dust covered everything. Dust spotted her cheeks reddish brown. It covered her hands in red dust mittens. She took a last swipe at a stunted sunflower. "How are you this morning, yellow fella?" she asked the sunflower.

"Oh, but I need some water," Lindy answered in a sunflower-high voice.

"I'll water you at sundown, yellow fella," she told the flower.

She tied her wiper around her waist. Her tank top and jeans were dusty. Lindy climbed up on the old wood fence and shook her head at their pie-shaped field. "Don't think the corn will make it," she called over to her dad.

"Lindy, stop your dawdling and come on here," he said back.

"Coming!"

She skipped, barefooted, to the side yard, where her dad worked at his garden-a-chance. "Shielded part way by the house," he'd once told her, "it is chance a garden will grow."

"I'll dig the hole, Lindy," he said now. "You put the baby plant in. Keep it straight and steady while I pour on the *gravy*."

"Gravy! Funny," laughed Lindy.

Her dad worked with the watering can. He poured a skinny stream of water — gravy — down over the young tomato plant, careful not to spill a drop. Lindy held it up with the tips of her fingers. She watched as the gravy dribbled down in the dust. Then, bracing the plant with one hand, she shoved the soil into the hole around it. The dirt was as fine as powder. She smoothed it around until the little plant stood by itself. Already it wilted over at the top.

"*Ka-choo!*" Lindy sneezed. Dust rose around them, reddening the light. "I don't know . . . ," she said.

"Well . . . and if it rains . . . ," her dad said, wistfully. Hope hung there between them.

"*And if it rains,*" Lindy sang, "*I get me some shoes and a dress-up all blue and pink and yellow, with flowers.*"

She leaned way back and smiled at the blue sky.

All was still. Lindy watched Mamalou come out to sweep

the tumbledown porch. Mamalou was the name she'd given her mother, who was Louise Esther. Lindy looked off as far as she could see beyond Mamalou, down the road, until the road dipped out of sight and the hard-time town of Osfield started. She frowned. "Feel a north breeze just so cool," Lindy told her dad. "Which way is north again?"

"Over my shoulder is north," he said. "But Lindy, there's no kind of breeze. Haven't ever known such blue sky."

Mamalou worked her way down the steps, sweeping the dust into neat piles.

"So little rain all the time now," Lindy's dad said.

"I never have seen more than a little rain," Lindy told him.

"When it comes down like a cloudburst, it's a lot," said her dad.

"Cloudburst!" said Lindy. "What would that be like?"

"Like the sky is opening up," he said.

"Like a river pouring down from above," said Mamalou, hearing them, all was so still. "Like buckets and buckets of just the longest rain-fella you ever saw in your life!"

"Is that true? It can rain like that?" asked Lindy, gazing at Mamalou, then back to her dad. She imagined a rain-fella, long and dark across the blue sky.

"It sure can," her dad answered. "But it hasn't rained like that in three years."

"I don't 'member three years," she said.

Her dad laughed. "You were so little then. There's just enough rain now to keep a minute of it down in the well."

"A minute of rain," she murmured, thinking about it. She imagined she heard a minute ticking raindrops, as she and her dad labored down the row.

Mamalou busied her broom over. She watched as they finished one short row. "Swept the porch," she told them, "and I swept the yard."

"Humm," Lindy's dad said.

Mamalou gazed at the yard where small clumps of grass struggled to grow. Most of the yard was dry, packed ground.

"Looking like pancakes, is the yard," said Lindy to her. "See, it cracks around into little cakes?"

"I see," said Mamalou. "I would give you pancakes to eat if I could. But I am all out of cornmeal."

Lindy pictured syrup spilling over pancakes. Her mouth watered; then the corners turned down a moment. But she never asked for what they didn't have. As was her way, she broke into a grin. "I don't mind my beans and gravy," she told Mamalou.

"Wish there was better," said her dad.

"Well, if it rains . . . ," Mamalou began. She let that fresh, watery thought go. "Think we are whistling in the wind," she said.

"What is that, whistling?" asked Lindy.

"Planting dry is useless work, what it means," said Mamalou. "I traded my cornmeal for tomato plants at market; had a taste for big tomatoes."

"But if it rains . . . ," said Lindy.

"These bitty plants will be ready for it," her dad finished.

Mamalou shook her head. She locked the broom like a flagstaff against her shoulder, rolled her hands in her apron, and went off into the house.

Lindy and her dad bent to their work, Lindy on one side of the row and her dad on the other. All at once, granules from the hard ground seemed to rise and jump along. Larger pieces of grit bounced up and rolled.

Lindy laughed. "Funny!" she said.

"What's funny?" asked her dad.

"Jumping dirt," said Lindy. "It's dancing."

"Huh," her dad said, only half listening. He lifted his head, looked toward the back of the land where there used to be a stream. Most rain came from there, from the south. The day was clear there beyond the streambed. Blue sky and no wind.

"Pretty sky," Lindy said. She had turned around, following his gaze.

Her dad said, "huh" again and, "Wouldn't mind to see a cloud come up."

"Is there always rain in a cloud?" she asked.

By way of an answer, her dad pointed to their work. She held the baby plant and covered its roots. But she was watching the grit dancing along.

"Funny-funny," Lindy said. And made a singsong. *"Gritty-funny, funny-gritty, sunny day!"*

"You like turning things 'round," her dad told her.

She grinned and turned herself all the way around. "I do!"

Lindy closed her eyes, leaning her head on her dad's shoulder a moment. She could feel the sun all over her. "I'm a baked potato," she told him.

Her dad laughed at that. She opened her eyes and sat up. That quickly, the day had changed. Maybe change had been creeping up on them. There were a whole lot of birds going by up in the air. Going by so fast, squawking. Just a big flock of them. And then, more change was coming. "Well, for — Dad?"

"Huh?" he said. "Lindy, hold the plant for me."

"But Dad, it's a wall." She looked over his shoulder, behind him.

"What is a wall, Lindy?" he asked.

"Dad, it's all brown and high! Dad, it's . . . it's coming!"

Her dad spun around. For a moment he simply stared northward. His mouth fell open. He took her hand, then, and started toward the house. "Come," he said, almost calmly.

All had grown quiet. There was a wall moving toward them from the north. It was not believable, but on it came.

Great numbers of birds had got out of the way of it. Around Lindy and her dad, grit and soil bounced and rolled toward it.

"Dad, it's like a great big wall-a-cloud. Is it if-it-rains?" asked Lindy. And then, "Dad! There's a stick running against the wall."

"What?" her dad said. He squinted hard to see. "Well, I'll be . . ." He saw. It did look like a stick figure was pressed to the wall and trying to run. But it was no stick. And that was no wall, although it looked like one.

"Never have seen a stick running. Never have seen a wall so high moving," said Lindy.

"No, child," her dad said. "It's a storm-a-dust. It's— Come on, Lindy, get in the house!"

Her dad pulled her fast. She flew off her feet. "Dad!" she said, and he eased up on her arm. But the grit was stinging her legs. The sky looked different now. No longer blue, it had turned gray. The air became harder to breathe. Bits of dusty ground went up Lindy's nose. *"Ka-choo! Ka-choo!"* she sneezed.

She and her dad clambered up the porch. Mamalou stood in the door, looking out to the north. "Goodness. Goodness," she said. "There's somebody . . . ," Mamalou began.

They watched what was coming against the wall. "It's bigger than a stick now," said Lindy.

"Looks like some fella," said Mamalou.

As the wall came closer, they could hear it swoosh with air and wind. The stick-fella ran about half a quarter-mile before the wall of dust. His shadowy, stick arms moved like pinwheels. His long legs scissored, in a hurry to cut out of there.

"Inside!" Lindy's dad urged her and Mamalou. They all went in. Quickly, Mamalou wet tatter cloths at the washstand and wrung them out. She handed a wet rag to Lindy and one to Lindy's dad. He stood with the door open just far enough for him to see out as the storm came on.

The air was hot and still outside. It was boiling inside. Lindy saw the sweat drip from her dad's face. Saw his eyes seem to run, even though he stood unmoving.

Mamalou closed all the windows. With her wet tatter cloth over her shoulder, she stuffed more tatters along the windowsills.

"Mamalou, what are you doing? Why are you in a hurry?" Lindy asked. "What must I do with this, my rag-a-wet?"

Mamalou stopped a moment. "You hold the tatter to your mouth. You'll see," Mamalou explained. "Stay close, Lindy! And we must keep the storm outside with these cloths at the windowsills."

Lindy heard deep, loud sound. She looked out the window. "The wall! It's bigger than big!" she cried. It loomed, scary, at the far end of the field. Now the world around them was misty-dusty.

Somebody came tripping onto the porch. Her dad held the door open as a spindly somebody came through. Somebody full of dust. Quickly her dad shut the door.

"Stick-fella!" Lindy said. She stared. A stranger. He was covered rusty. He stumbled and fell on the floor, coughing.

There was so much going on. Lindy saw their field get wiped away in a red mist. Now the house inside was hazy with a rusty fog. The dust filled the front room. It fell on the linoleum and spread over the white lace tablecloth that had been sewn many times by Lindy and Mamalou, washed and starched, too, so it looked new.

Now Lindy watched the tablecloth get covered with brown. She began coughing, just like the stick-fella on the floor. She held the moist rag to her mouth and sat down at the table.

Only a few minutes had passed. But outside, it was dark as night. The wall never hit them. It was like it went right through them. Dust came in, sifting right through the wallboards. There was wind sound, and grit sound slapping the house. It felt as if the house lifted, then held itself tight.

Lindy couldn't think of anything funny to say. Couldn't smile. She felt gritty. She couldn't get her breath. She made fists. Her chest heaved. A sob rose from her throat.

Her dad was there beside her. "Breathe through the tatter," he told her. "That's it; put it over your nose. Breathe, child." And she did, easier now.

The stick-fella sprawled on the floor. He tried to get up. Mamalou and Lindy's dad took hold of him. They set him upright in a chair. Mamalou had an old dish towel wetted, and she helped him wipe his eyes and face. The stick-fella was a boy. Long and thin as a skinny rail. Spindly, too, and the color of pale wood under the grime of dust.

"You are a long, dusty somebody," Lindy said. "Dad, see? It's a tall boy!" She forgot about crying now. She coughed a few times, but breathing through the tatter made it better.

"Reckon he is older than you, too," her dad said. "What do they call you, son?" he asked the tall boy.

"Tall Boy!" Lindy whispered. And he heard her.

"That's not . . . ," he sputtered, spit, and coughed. He struggled to breathe. ". . . *my name*," he finished. His voice was a cooling breeze, after he had cleared his throat of dust.

He took some swallows of water from a cup Mamalou gave him. Outside was hard wind sound. He put the cup down and held the dish towel to his nose. Then, he wiped his arms and neck with it; wiped his head and ears and hands. He wiped his shirt and dungarees, and made mud streaks clear down his front. His movement made a cloud of dust rise around him. He tried to take a deep breath, but it got caught in a cough. Sweat broke out on his cleaned forehead and made it glisten. He took another sip of water and breathed hard. His hands were shaking. Lindy saw them.

Mamalou took another damp tatter and held it by its end. She let it hang down into the small cloud of dust the stick-fella had raised. Slowly she swung the rag and lifted it up and down.

Right before their eyes, Mamalou wiped up the cloud on the rag. All around the room, she wiped rusty dust off the air. She finished when she had done all she could to help them breathe.

"Where do you come from? Where are your people?" Mamalou asked the stick-fella.

The tall boy breathed hard and did not answer at once.

"You ran a long way?" asked her dad.

"Must've wore you out," Mamalou said.

"Did your people get lost in the wall?" Lindy asked. She was the first one of them the boy looked at.

Mamalou and Lindy's dad stared at the boy as though he were an odd-fella. Lindy didn't think so. "Why is it so bad out?" Lindy asked him.

The tall boy looked around. He saw the dust seeping in.

"The floor is covered, look," she told them.

"It gets in everything," Mamalou said.

"You will eat dust for a while," her dad said.

But Lindy was watching the long, tall young'un. "Talk! Why don't you say more?" she asked him.

"I will," he said. "Was afraid I'd start a coughing fit." And then, "Are you the only child?"

Lindy nodded. She thought he sounded fresh, the way her dad said once the stream had sounded. She said, "Someday Mamalou will have me a little brother. How old are you, tall boy?"

They all stared at him. "He can talk," Lindy told.

"Course he can," Mamalou said.

"And your name?" her dad said to the stick-fella.

"It's Tall Boy!" Lindy said, then covered her mouth, ashamed of herself.

"No," the boy said. "It's Drylongso."

"What?" asked Lindy's dad and Mamalou.

"Drylongso," he said again. The name echoed in Lindy's thoughts. *'longso. Drylongso.* "Funny *name!*" Lindy said.

Drylongso looked away. And she was sorry she'd spoken out.

He looked back at them. "Ma says there was drought like this before," he said. "It lasted so long, folks thought it was just ordinary. Dry so long, it was common, like everyday. See, drought came to be Dry-long-so."

"And you, Drylongso . . . ," Mamalou began.

He said, "Ma says she dreamed a hard dust time was coming. Another Dry-long-so. Then, I was born. Ma said, 'He comes into the world, and a time of no clouds will come after him. Where he goes,' she said, 'life will grow better.'"

"Is that right? Well, I'll be," said Lindy's dad.

"And the drought came," said the tall boy, "and long been here, just as ordinary as everyday."

"Drylongso," said Lindy's dad.

"It's a drought for sure," said Mamalou. "And you came here running before the dust wall, Drylongso."

"Drylongso," murmured Lindy.

The house braced itself as a fresh wave of dust hit. Grit scraped and scrabbled at the windows. No matter that Mamalou had covered cracks where she could, dust got in everyplace.

Lindy laughed at her dad. His face was a reddish mask with eyeholes, nose and mouth holes. She brushed away a dusting from the cabinet mirror and saw her own face. She, too, had a mask on. She made its eyes cross. She made it grin, showing teeth.

Drylongso said, "Dust goes where it pleases when it pleases."

"I wish it would go *away!*" Lindy said.

"Pa says that if folks would stop plowing where they shouldn't, the dust would settle down," said Drylongso.

"That so?" said Lindy's dad. "We've no tractors here. Now we use an old push plow. We turn the ground by hand. It's been like turning dust over."

Drylongso said, "We saw the wall coming from far away; me and my family started running. A big dust swirl caught us.

I heard them calling me, but I was choking. See, the driver of us field folks couldn't see. Panic got him, and he let us out."

"And you got separated?" Lindy's dad asked.

"I got apart from them," said the boy.

"I'd be afraid without my dad," said Lindy. But they were listening to Drylongso.

"Thistles," the boy said, all at once. "Sunflowers. Plant some, let them spread. They hold down the soil until the grasses grow here again, my pa says. That great wall that came upon all us — don't you see what it was?"

"It was like the earth reared up," said Lindy's dad.

Drylongso's eyes lit up. He nodded, eagerly. "Earth's not made to heave up so, but to lie down. The ground stands up to teach folks not to plow the grasslands."

"Seems so," said Lindy's dad. "There was a dust storm once, started in New Mexico and traveled whole as far as Washington, D.C. Folks had overused the land. Made it rise up."

"Wasn't that the 1930s?" asked Mamalou. "This is 1975; we know more."

Drylongso said, politely, "Pa says we can make plenty, and we think there will always be plenty. He says droughts come about every twenty years. And this here is another one."

Lindy's dad nodded, said, "From the 1890s, and the 1910s, 1930s, 1950s . . ."

"And now, the 1970s," said Drylongso. "Drought will come again in the 1990s, my pa says."

"Aren't you afraid, all by yourself?" asked Lindy. Her eyes were tearing. She coughed. Mamalou gave her some water to drink and put her arm around Lindy's shoulder. Made Lindy feel better.

Drylongso told a joke then, looking right at Lindy, too. "A pilot's plane got stuck in a black blizzard-a-dust, thousands of feet up. He bailed out. Had to shovel his way clear to the ground. When he got down, he carved a car for himself, blizzard black of dust, and drove away."

Her dad laughed at that.

"Is that true?" asked Lindy.

"No, but it's funny," said Mamalou.

They stayed in the house with Drylongso. All day, wind blew. Darkness came and went. Cast over the air was a peculiar bluish color caused by the filtering dust. They all stared out at an eerie blue world. Then they got used to it. Mamalou began making soup for them. They would have bread she had baked. They needn't go to town unless they ran out of water. Unless the well ran dry. Long rattle-car ride to there.

The storm let up, but it didn't stop. "We'd better go out," said Lindy's dad to Drylongso. "Run clothesline to the shed and from there to the field. So Mamalou and Lindy can walk about safely in case bad goes to worst."

"Okay," said Drylongso. Then he asked, "Is there a stream nearby?"

"There was a stream, long dry now," said Lindy's dad. "Nothing left to it but the bed of it."

"You will stay with us, of course," Mamalou told Drylongso.

"I forgot to ask if I could," said Drylongso.

"No need in asking. Course you can stay," Mamalou said.

"You are bigger than me," Lindy said to Drylongso. "I'll let you be my brother anyhow." They all laughed at that.

"Tell me your name," said Drylongso.

"Lindy!" Lindy said.

"It's Linn Dahlia," said Mamalou. "But Lindy is quicker." She smiled.

"And just as pretty," said Lindy's dad.

"And easy for me," said Lindy.

"Okay, Lindy, my sister," said Drylongso. "See? I'm not by myself."

Lindy smiled to everyone.

Through the night, she heard wind and grit strike the windows. Once, she woke to a dead calm outside. In the morning, she awakened to dull sunlight. The windowsill was covered in dust, as was the straight chair and the bedcovers. Lindy sat up. The only clean place was on her pillow where her head had lain.

"Mamalou!" she wailed. Mamalou came quickly to help and comfort her.

"Dust is in everything," Lindy said later as she ate her bread and molasses with a cup of milk. "Storm gone?" she asked.

"Long gone to bother somewheres else," said Drylongso. He sat down at the morning table.

"Didn't think about you!" Lindy said. She'd forgotten all about him.

"Thanks a lot!" he said, smiling. "Want to go and see outside?"

Lindy jumped up from the table. "Yes."

Outside, at the edge of the porch, Lindy saw a whole new world of dust.

"Now these would be white drifts if it'd been a snow-storm," said Drylongso.

Dust had drifted up over half of the porch. It had drifted over the steps. Drifted across the shed, covering the door latch, slanting upward.

Every window had little drifts in the corners. Their pie-shaped field had been swept clean of soil. What was showing was bare, hardpan, hard scrabble. What had been young corn lay flattened, dead or dying, drowning in dust. Dust shifted as high as the fenceposts around the field. It drifted in waves across the road into town.

"A lot of somebody's topsoil," Drylongso said. "A whole bunch of farms without any ground to plant."

"All our baby 'matoes is covered!" Lindy whimpered.

"Well, don't cry," he said. "Let me tell you about this man. Well, he came along on his horse after a dust storm. He saw a ten-gallon hat sitting atop a dust drift by a fencepost. Man went over there on his horse, reached over, picked up the hat. Only to find there was a head under it. It was another fellow, see, dust drift clear to his shoulders, just his head free there under the hat. Man on the horse says to the fellow, says, 'Well, do you want me to help you out of that dirt?' Man under the hat says, 'No, I'll just be a minute, catchin' my breath. Just restin' awhile, sittin' here on my mule.'"

It took a second, but then Lindy smiled and laughed.

"See, the other fellow has a mule under him buried in the dust," Drylongso explained.

"I got it the first time," said Lindy.

"Well, okay, you're real smart, too!" said Drylongso.

The storm had ended. But there was wind, and the dust floated around as high as the trees. The town's power had shorted out from blowing dust, and there was no electricity. Other places, phone lines were down. They all walked around in a haze, with blue sky sometimes showing. The sunlight got through a little bit. They felt hot and gritty all the time. Lindy helped Mamalou wash and clean everything inside. They swept the dust outside.

After her dad dug out the shed, he and Drylongso got out the tools.

"We're your helpers, Mamalou and me," said Lindy.

They carried everything down to the once-a-stream. Drylongso said there was lots that could be done there.

"How does he know?" Lindy asked Mamalou.

"He seems to know things," Mamalou told her. "Says there won't be hard rain until the end of the decade, until the eighties."

"You said this was 1975," Lindy said. Lindy counted to herself and said, "How do we get to the eighties?"

"The best way we can, Lindy," said Mamalou.

They laid down a hoe, a mattock, two shovels, and a pick along the streambed where the dust seemed to have passed on. Mamalou and Lindy sat down beside the tools, watching Drylongso. Lindy's dad took up the hoe and leaned on it awhile. Drylongso was standing in the streambed, shaded by spindly trees. They were young, like whips with a few droopy, dust-covered leaves.

Drylongso crossed his hands over his chest, touching his shoulders. He had something odd resting on his feet. He was looking down at his feet at the thing like a forked whip of sapling. He lifted his head, looking up into bright haze. Dust around him in the light and air swirled with the breeze and then seemed to fall below his knees. Drylongso stood then in clear air.

"All the clothes I got, I wear," he said, sounding older. "What I own is in my pockets." He put one hand in his pocket, brought it out, and showed a handful of seeds. He put the other hand in the other pocket. He brought out more seeds and small potato cuts. "These are good for planting," he said. "Seeds have been cured in clean cloth under the best moonshine.

"You plant corn on the full moon," said Drylongso. "It will grow short and the ears full. Plant potatoes in this last of April on the nights of dark when the moon is going down. There's three dark nights before the new moon. We got corn, potatoes, tomatoes, and beans. I give them over to you to grow."

Mamalou took it all and rolled it up in her apron.

"Don't you need the seeds?" Lindy's dad asked Drylongso.

"You need them," Drylongso said. "My pa will gather seed for the next planting."

"How do you know?" asked Mamalou.

He looked at her. "Well, because my pa will keep on just regular," he said.

"Just ordinary," agreed Mamalou, smiling.

"Just like everyday," said Lindy's dad, chuckling.

Lindy's face broke into a grin. "Dry-long-so!" she said.

"Right you are," said Drylongso. "Well, it's what goes on like clockwork, like the seasons."

Lindy's dad asked, "Is that a divining rod at your feet?"

"It's a dowser, yes," Drylongso said.

"A dowser," Lindy said. "What is it?"

"Some call it a dowsing rod, too," Mamalou said. "He finds water with it. My uncle King could do that dowsing."

"You believe in it, son — that stick can divine us water?"

Drylongso heaved a sigh. He said, "It's what my pa showed me he couldn't do, but his dad could. And I can."

"I'm afraid to use what little water is left in the well without boiling it first," said Mamalou.

"Around here was a stream," said Drylongso. "So there is water, way down. But what I want to find is a spring."

"Underground," said Lindy's dad, shaking his head.

Drylongso looked shyly at Lindy's dad. But his eyes were bright as sparkles. "Yep," he said, and that was all.

He walked off a ways by himself. He had taken up his dowser. He held one stem of the stick on his left hand under the thumb. He put the other stem of the stick in his mouth. He moved up and down the streambed away from them.

"Strange," said Mamalou, softly. "But I've seen it done like that."

"I don't know if I believe in this," said Lindy's dad.

"I believe," said Lindy. "Drylongso. I believe."

Every now and then, the dowser would jerk down toward the ground. Then it would go back up straight from Drylongso's mouth. He turned around, came back toward them. As he neared them, the dowser began to bend peculiarly. As he walked, it was pulling down and down until the tip pointed straight down. He was past them now. But not far. Down toward the far side of the streambed. Down where there were weeds and climbing ground.

Drylongso turned, faced the climbing ground. The dowser swayed to the right, then straight down. The dowser looked as if it were pointing. It did not tremble. It was as if the forked stick knew there was something underground. Whatever was down there had the stick in a steady pull.

They could see Drylongso. He turned to look at them. Lindy's dad went over there. Then Lindy and Mamalou got up and walked over across the once-a-stream to the far side. There the land rose to a higher bank.

"Found what you were looking for, then," said Lindy's dad.

Drylongso nodded. He rested the forked stick on his feet. "Now we have to pick and shovel."

"But first, we ought to make shallow trenches across the streambed — you see that?" asked Lindy's dad.

"Yes," Drylongso said. "You can forget about your field without topsoil. I say plant down here."

"There's not going to be rain, you think?" asked Mamalou.

Drylongso nodded. "My pa calls it 'drouth' time, a time of thirst. It will be a long time going."

Lindy's dad sighed and studied his shoes.

He wiped his neck on his handkerchief. He looked at the boy, Drylongso. How do you trust a boy? his look seemed to say. Then, he made up his mind.

"Let's start," he said.

"You mean to plant down here?" asked Mamalou. "Well, the stream might flood."

"Yes, but not for years," said Lindy's dad.

"It will be work," she said. "I'm not saying I won't help." She smiled.

"I'll help," Lindy said.

"Well, then, we can surely start right now," said Lindy's dad.

Lindy followed her dad and Mamalou. Drylongso and her dad agreed how the labor was to be done. First they would trench the land from high ground to low. Then they would prepare the low ground and as much of the streambed as seemed good to cultivate, following the streambed curve. They must have it done in a few days, for the planting times were nearly over.

As the day turned, they used pick and shovel, mattock and hoe and trenched the low land. "Easy enough to trench ground that still has some lumps to it," Mamalou said to Lindy.

"It feels cool, some," said Lindy, "on my bare toes!" She wore no shoes, since they would only get full of dust.

"Cool means there is faint moisture," said her dad.

"But when does the dowser find water?" asked Lindy.

"It already did," said Drylongso.

"Where's the water?" she asked him.

Drylongso smiled shyly but said no more.

They worked. After the trenches were done, they started in clearing the lowland. They picked and mattock-hoed the hard places. Drylongso took the shovel and turned the earth as deeply as he could. Lindy's dad took up a hoe, chopping the turned ground. Mamalou came behind him and raked everything. What wouldn't smooth out, she raked to the side, out of the way.

They didn't finish the first day. "Best not to try too large a piece," said Lindy's dad. "Thirty, forty feet long may be good. And as wide as the streambed and the lowland. Nice-sized, that we can handle. It's late in the season anyhow."

"Time for corn, maybe ten rows," Drylongso said. "Tomatoes will grow. You can plant beans by your corn."

"Want to hear a joke?" asked Lindy's dad.

"Sure," both Lindy and Drylongso said at the same time.

"Tell you about this farmer I know. Asked him did he plant by the moon. And he said, 'No, takes years to get there. I like to plant down here on earth!'"

Drylongso laughed. Lindy almost got it. "The moon is far, far up," she said, seriously.

They all laughed at that. She grinned. Her way was always to make folks laugh. She let the joke go.

They prepared the land. It took most of three days working all day. They cut some few dried weeds, some brush, down. Mamalou raked them to the middle of places, and Lindy stacked them. They lit a fire to them. They made the piles burn slowly. They added whatever leaves there were under the trees. All of it burned down to ashes. Then Mamalou and Lindy hoed cooled ashes under the soil, turning it. Ashes made the soil richer. But the soil hadn't been worked, and so it was rich enough to grow things well.

And by the fourth day, Lindy woke up late. She'd been working so. Everybody was down to the bottom by the time she got there. They were planting.

"Wait for me!" she told them.

Drylongso opened his hand.

There were seeds on his palm. "Here's for a pepper patch, Lindy," he said.

"Pepper is black," she told him. "You shaker it out."

He laughed, handing Lindy the seeds. "Forgot I had them in my shirt pocket. This is green bell pepper when it grows. You'll see, come July or August. Plant them in a row, doesn't matter how close. No need to worry, they grow thick as kin."

He made a short row.

Lindy dropped in the seeds, close as kin in a church pew or peas in a pod. Drylongso covered them over with soil. She thought, *You are my kin, too!*

"Do we water them now?" she asked.

"We will," said Drylongso.

His dowser now lay on the high ground. They all went over there. Stood there. Drylongso took up the pick. Lindy's dad swung the mattock. Mattock was shaped like a pick, only its head was broad on one side and pointed on the other.

The swinging of the tools made the air rush. The dust rose as ground broke away. Lindy stepped back. So did Mamalou. Lindy held Mamalou's hand. She winced each time the mattock struck the high bank. Mamalou blinked when the pick caught and pulled the land, tearing into it.

They broke the high bank down to the ground. Then, they dug below the ground, down and down, two feet or more. They deepened the trenches the same level. By the time they had finished, the hole in the ground seemed dark and a mystery to Lindy.

Still holding Mamalou's hand, she peered into it. "What seeds will you put there?" she asked Drylongso.

"Lindy, don't you get it?" he asked her.

"No!" she said. "It's because I'm little!" she wailed. "I don't get it!"

"It's nothing, now don't get upset," Drylongso told her. He put his hand along one sidewall of the hole. He let his hand play along it as though searching for a heartbeat. Then, he straightened. He took up the shovel and swung it hard at the side of the hole.

And there came water. Not a lot, at first, but a trickling and then a steadying, like a spring.

"Water's been there all the time," Lindy's dad said.

"You just have to know to find it," Drylongso said.

"Most folks can't find it," said Mamalou.

"But will it last?" asked Lindy's dad.

Drylongso said, "It's springwater, cut off and covered up this long, going someplace else but here. It probably will flow here awhile as regular as can be."

They watched the water. Then Lindy's dad found a good piece of wood that he chopped out and put under the spring across the hole to the first trench. They made cross canals from one trench to the other. They made one narrow canal to one side along the high length of the bottomland.

"Now you can cut off any trench or any canal and make the water go where you want it," Drylongso said.

"Yes, you trap it by damming it," Lindy's dad said. "If the water comes faster, it may well work."

"It'll work," Drylongso said, quietly.

All that day, Lindy kept an eye on the new plant ground with her dad. Sometimes, she forgot about Drylongso, so surprised was she by the running water.

"It's the sweetest water, Lindy. Want to taste it?" asked her dad.

"Yes!" she said.

He had hooked a tin cup to his belt. He took it up and filled it half-full of water. When Lindy drank, it was so cold, it took her breath.

"Fresh!" she managed. "Cold!"

"Good!" Her dad laughed.

It seemed to Lindy that the plantings came up almost overnight. She watched them to see if she could catch them growing.

"They grow when your back is turned," said Mamalou. And no matter how quickly Lindy turned toward them, she never caught them growing.

One day, Lindy's dad and Drylongso went into town. It took a long time to start the car. That's what woke Lindy — the car muttering and fussing.

"Found work all this week digging out the rails," said her dad when he came back at evening.

She had her feet in the springwater and was daydreaming about stringbeans on the table and tomatoes and corn in a few months, and her own pepper patch. It was later, at dusk, that she called, "Drylongso, where did you get? C'mere." Drylongso never came.

"He found a ride out from town," said Mamalou at supper.

"He had to go, Lindy, catch up with his mom and dad," her dad told her.

"He's my brother!" was all she could think to say.

"He's your pretend brother and your real friend," said Mamalou.

"He didn't say good-bye to me!"

"He thought it would be easier," her dad said. "Lindy, don't take on so. It was time he got going to where he belonged."

"You are mean, Dad!" hollered Lindy.

"Lindy, all of us are sorry to see him go."

"But remember," said Mamalou, "when he was born his mama said that where he *goes*, life will grow better."

Lindy looked at her. "I don't get it," she said.

"Drylongso came running before the dust wall," said her dad.

"And after the dust, he *goes*. And he went. The plant-ings — life — grows!" said Mamalou.

"Oh!" said Lindy. "They . . . grow . . . better every day!"

"We'll miss Drylongso," said Mamalou.

Lindy would miss him all the time, in a lump in her throat and a sad place inside her.

All the next day, she watched over the plantings while her dad worked shoveling mountains of dust drifts off the railroad tracks. All was so quiet without Drylongso. But it felt good to Lindy to wiggle her toes in the springwater while Mamalou made sure all of the little canals fed the trenches alongside the plantings. It was not until afternoon when the sun was on a slant that Lindy wandered along the lowland.

And found Drylongso's dowser rod. "Mamalou! Look!" she called, holding it up.

"Well, I'll be!" said Mamalou. "He left it for you."

"He did?" asked Lindy.

"Course he did," said Mamalou. "Nice of him, too."

Lindy played with the dowser. She skipped with it. She dipped it into a little canal. But she couldn't make it point the way Drylongso had.

She imagined with the dowser. "Make clouds," she told it. "Bring rain!" She pointed it at the sky. Nothing happened. Lindy smiled. "I made rain someplace else. Mamalou," she called, "I made rain in California!"

Mamalou had a good laugh at that.

Lindy wandered some more. She always ended back wherever Mamalou was working. "Find anything else?" asked Mamalou.

"It's what I'm gonna find," said Lindy. Suddenly her face broke open like sunshine. "Some day . . . ," she said.

"Some day, what?" asked Mamalou.

". . . I'll find Drylongso with the dowser."

"And that will surely be *some* day," said Mamalou.

"I made it rain all over California with the dowser rod," she told her dad. He tucked her in to sleep.

"Some parts out there always need a lot of rain, too," he answered. "Good night, Lindy."

"'Night," she said. She lay in bed, imagining Drylongso leaping over dust drifts. Dry so long, she was thinking.

"Wherever Drylongso *goes*, life grows better," she murmured. He didn't say good-bye . . . because . . .

Her eyes were closing. And then they opened wide.

"He's coming back," she said, out loud. But when?

He'll come when it's cool again, she decided. She imagined him running before a cloudburst. A soaking-wet, shivering rain-fella! He was laughing, running to their house, bringing a downpour.

Dry so long. So long, Drylongso. We'll plant some sunflowers, too. And I'll see you in the eighties.

Lindy's eyes closed. She slept.

AUTHOR'S NOTE

Severe drought in the United States generally occurs at regular twenty-year intervals. I have based the climate conditions in *Drylongso* on weather patterns that developed in the 1930s, the 1950s, and again in the 1970s. *Drylongso* takes place in 1975.

There were never the number of dust storms in the 1970s that there had been in the 1930s. But they did occur, and *Drylongso* contains one such event of nature during a long drought period. The story takes place west of the Mississippi River. However, drought can and does occur anywhere in America periodically, as the research shows.

The word *drylongso* was handed down from early generations of the African-American community during the Plantation Era. Its most likely origin is the creolized Gullah language and its geechee dialect from the Georgia Sea Islands. Gullah was the widespread black colloquial speech of the early generations of the era.

Drought came so often and for so long that it was viewed as something as regular as every day. It became known in the patois as dry-long-so. Later, drylongso came to mean ordinary. A person who was plain-featured was drylongso. And life, or a day, was boringly the same, and drylongso.

In this story, I have given drylongso a part-mythical quality and an embodiment. Drylongso is a youth imbued with simple human kindness. Not only does he personify drought, but he also represents the longing for rain. Finally, I have portrayed Drylongso as a folk hero. With the dowser as his talisman, he is fortune, destiny; he is the symbol of fate.

— VIRGINIA HAMILTON

The paintings in this book were done in pencil,
watercolor, and pastel on Arches watercolor paper.
The display type was set in Centaur with swash characters and
the text type in Berling by Thompson Type, San Diego, California.
Color separations by Bright Arts, Ltd., Singapore
Printed and bound by Tien Wah Press, Singapore
This book was printed on Arctic matte paper.
Production supervision by Warren Wallerstein and Ginger Boyer
Designed by Trina Stahl